PRESENT OR ACCOUNTED FOR

Poems by Manly Johnson

T0204714

COUNCIL OAK BOOKS

Council Oak Books
1350 East Fifteenth Street
Tulsa, Oklahoma 74120

Design by Carol Haralson & Carl Brune
Cover photo of Manly Johnson by Don Wheeler
Printed in the United States of America

Library of Congress Cataloging-in-Publication Data

Johnson, Manly.
    Present or accounted for : poems / by Manly Johnson.
        p.   cm.
    ISBN 0-933031-84-X : $9.95
    I. Title.
PS 3560.037979P74   1993
811' . 54--dc20   93-38697
                                                      CIP

Some of these poems appeared in the following:
Anecdotes of a Time and People (Hadassah Press), *Midland
Review, Nimrod, The Phoenix, All Morning in Her Eyes*
(riverrun press), *University of Tulsa Monogram #2.*
Grateful acknowledgement is made for permission to reprint.

For Francine,
Love, Spirit of the Place, & Celebrant

*When memory and anticipation are
completely absent, there is a complete
conformity to the average influence of the
immediate past . . . Such a situation
produces the activity of mere matter. . . .
Thus the universe is material in proportion
to the restriction of memory and
anticipation.*

WHITEHEAD
Essays in Science and Philosophy

The poems of this collection are based on the premise
that what you desire is revealed: myth — the telling
word, memory — the thinking back, that without
both we are signs not read, homeless in an empty
land, not knowing where we are, or who, or why. So
they begin with dreams of childhood, go on through
loves and loving, with a look at what are dear to us —
the earth, trees, sky, water, friends — and end with
questionings about those we have, in one way or
another, lost. As the forms of life are various, so the
poems themselves appear in a variety of forms. Like
the forms of life, they are subject to constant change,
arrested here as at a station, waiting to go on. The
consolation is that waiting makes the poem: it is read,
considered and, insofar as it is received, becomes a
small part of life.

C O N T E N T S

SPIRITS OF PLACES

PRESENT OR ACCOUNTED FOR

RUNES & CONJURINGS

Naming

I came in my dream to the elephant graveyard
where the great ones lie down with their kind.
Searching among the white bones, among mellow ivory,
I found, perched in windows of the hollow skulls,
creatures small as warblers, red, orange,
yellow, blue, and purple, singing.

They would not come to me, nor could I touch,
their song like squeaking and rumbling of whales heard
where I huddled, behind wire, small, dark as a roach, and
still.

I could not think what name they had,
I did not know to call them by their names.
But they knew mine, and sang as if for pleasure
all the names I own.

Morphy's Hands

Clock on its tall stand in moonlight
through the window curtain glows and winks its lid.
Hands there, and a scratchy voice.

Bright of night, dark chased into corners, huddles
under shed, not even the leaves quiver naked
beneath the walking moon, full in the fish pond's center.
Stars, stare! My angel fish sunk there, come up:
sing me, sing, and if you wrinkle that still water
with your snouts, make bubbles burst their music,
auntie doesn't care. Morphy's hands smooth out her face,
all the hairy moles, put flowers in her mousey breath
and make her hold me like she did.

The boat I ride beneath the window in the room is leaky,
shore is still and safe. Go in the walking moon, pulls
me by my eyes cold in the staring light with little moons.
The path is cold, grass is weeping where I step. Hide,
angel fish, the arbor's black and with its purple grapes
is falling on your heads! Sing for your lives—the moon
is falling too.
He wants the angel of the blind girl hanging on the wall
to keep him from the dark hole where the spiders live.
Smooth him with the feathers of its wing. Where is, he
asks, my chicken Goldie that you ate? The sandal on his
foot was what he wore, Greek as any Roman, his face

the look of flowers waiting and his eyes paced
through the lens and into now, the sepia tint
like afternoons in August when the light is slant.

Walks the shore to look for angel fish, their singing
in the bubbles of surf, hears crashing waves and roar
of trucks and still can't say what he wants to say
before the hunters' moon pours down its death white
beauty on the shattered water.

She Is No Poem

    Her petals scent the air
with fragrance more subtle
than theirs.

    Colors, indescribable
even through metaphor,
compare

    with morning's cool, evening's
warmer shades as lovely
is to fair.

    Her lines, irregular
as free verse, seem to chime
in pairs,

    as if the body's sonnet
closing there, made of its
affairs

    music. Any man would
be bound to the mast for
those airs

serene and ecstatic.
When singing out self's
myriads

she, angel in the same
space with distracting forces,
enthralls

the dullest of this wax-
eared clan, who play in one
staid chord

our minimalist loves.
Here I am bound to say
she is no poem.

The Girls

for Alexandra

The girls, ah the marvelous girls,
the gallant women, striding in their knee boots
in their jodhpurs—we cannot help them
when they will be thrown,
the girls, before their troubles start
—beyond daddy, brothers, and the vagrant lot
at corners, alleys, vacant fields—
sifting the golden sunlight through hair
they will some night let down from towers
for the climb of fresh-cheeked dolts
in jockey shorts and long-billed caps, grinning,
spinning out of moonlight the silver sheen
    of gown and veil and bridal sheets.

Astrid's Oklahoma Poems

They summon us
with the sound of her voice
slightly dented, as with beaten gold,
Latvian green and white beneath
a south-west warmth
of vowels and intonation,
with the look of her face
in Ivar's garden portrait,
sunlight livening the duskiness
of golden hair, the mouth's
double curve of melancholy and mirth,
with quiet lines of constancy
in motion, power of seas
that move their oceanic depths
through storms, serenely potent.

Even to this inland place
she brought the sturdy Latvian shore,
wind-blown and spare, on which
    the breakers beat,
shouting their wild, regular, muffled vowels
through the wind of this space and hawk-strewn sky.

They say, "we trek to find our fathers' bones"
when streams will flow again
and grass will grow and trees,

and trails of tears shed rain
over the green shield of Oklahoma.

Every utterance a washing of the words.
she hangs them out, and sends them
clean and fresh.
Whether Little Coon's Creek words
went home with him forever
matters—and his English words.
The English words and the Latvian words,
the Estonian words and the Irish.
With het tap toe quarters, she goes with us
when we leave the public house,
and gathers with us round the fires,
tells the stories of Vivia Locke
and Connie, Lightning Girl, Alene.

Out of a notebook thrown into the fire
—charms of the healer,
the soothsayer, the sorceress—
the old ones rise in shapes of smoke and flame,
they gather round us in the dusk,
they bring their gifts
of sun, and slanting rain,
growlings of distant thunder,
bird cries in the orchard,
alien tongues we cannot understand
but listen to as sung,
conjuring now in living light and sound
here, in Ireland, or in Latvia, her.

Naked Self

"THE BODY IS THE GREAT POEM."
Wallace Stevens

Bearing proud
    she strides her ways
a dik-dik's prancing grace
    more than Salome's veils,
diaphanous, reveal her elegant limbs'
    unconsciously enchanting tricks.

Bearing steady,
    steel and gem stone,
on which the unchecked ticking
    of timely intention moves its wheel,
in the bone resprung
    made ready by the month's turn.

Baring innocent,
    without seductive wiles,
compels assent
    to the slenderest form of function
whose only ornament
    is naked self,
purest of styles.

Cigarette

i

In your mouth
   is the bitter taste of nicotine
I am addicted to.

ii

   The smoke
curls
      from your mouth. . .
        I watch,
          envious.

iii

   Smoke is a kiss
we exchange
in the chambers
   of our lungs.

iv

    The smoke curls
into a question:
    How many cigarettes
are left to us?

v

Death touched you
   tentatively. . .
they took
   what he touched.

I am not jealous:
   all the rest
      is mine.

The Venue of Worms

"THE POET MAKES SILK DRESSES OUT OF WORMS"
Wallace Stevens

St. George had business with a worm
whose jet breath had burnt many a brand
before the Knight's
severed his fuel line.

And that one's father
in the Garden coiled silkily
to insinuate a tongue
slick with honey
into the most secret parts
of our mother.

Now in this wormy world
remembering all the beasts
that move their slow thighs,
around Jerusalem
we raise our silken tents.

Sleep, sleep, beloved woman
into your dream
our words enter, plumb
in your womb flowers
the poem of the world.

Two Islands

We are struck by Enku
to see the grain growing
in wood cut off from life,
as if the sap slowing

from tap root took renewed
life from chisel's striking
to prepare Fudo,
Buddhist -Shinto fireking,

for worship in mountain
ritual exercises—
bathing in icy falls'
hardy paradises,

chanting incantations
hanging from cliff edges
to enact life's rebirth,
subsisting on sedges.

He hewed fire-clad, fierce-faced
Fudo as one might fight
against evil forces
with energy's insight,

emblazoned on surface
the sign of his ax's
power and his chisel's
keenness, the sole axis

between Enku's body
and his raging spirit—
not for his own profit
or pleasure endure it,

so rapid, decisive
his strokes no correction
was needed or wanted—
to make his election

of metaphysical
powers, his vision
as plain as the surface,
a clear-cut decision

to be first in saying,
as he was in climbing
Uchira and Usu,
there could be no miming

of virtue or evil.
Toward bodies, specific
in range of qualities
malign to pacific

and their imperfect ends,
we are struck by Enku.

*The "two islands" are Japan and Ireland. Enku was a
seventeenth century monk who sculpted more than one hundred
thousand Buddhas. The Rionnaird Tri N-ard is a medieval Irish
verse form.*

The Preppy

Is it just a matter of style—
how the collar is worn, the pant leg straight,
the penny loafer and the boat shoe—
or is it more a matter of how the mind
is predisposed to know: those who do and those who don't?

With the preppy's elegant slippered foot goes the hand,
that rounded oblong script, the matter neatly arrayed
in unimpeachable categories.
The voice too, under the buttoned-down collar
delivering itself of certainties,
no points left free to flop around,
each symbol hard-edged as a diamond,
and every form pressed out as if in Flint,
reproduceable on demand.

Pain, says the preppy, is what we avoid
by choosing—dependable as it is—the rack of ages.
On this rack they found their church.
It conquers the world:
we are not surprised to see in the tropics
button-down collars over naked breasts,
the chino loincloth hanging straight,
without cuffs, and northward, pink parkas
made chic with real baby seals
skewered to the left pocket.

The preppy is father, pater, padre, pope,
left-over authority, sans beard, sans paddle,
but holding the book like a torch,
shaped up to be a flame by day,
a column of smoke by night,
at all other times a pillar of salt,
turned in to himself, astringent, cristaline:
when tried, one is tempted to take a large pinch.

Naked, the preppy appears un-preppy,
hardly a thing buttoned down,
not even the upper lip,
mobile as Huck Finn's
spitting watermellon seeds,
the pubic hair arranged in curls—surprise—
not herringbone at all,
and all the little animals down the drain:
a real, live human being, at his best—
a fate others might envy—in the shower.

Out of the Sea

Out of the sounding throat of mountainous seas
words never came that sent them:
Waves muttering come, come, constantly shattered
on rocks, stating in foam, stay with us, stay with us,
as if the spume of a thousand rocky leviathans
with swelling of moist waters articulated desire,
a sickness of longing
for the sea as home.   For the sea was home,
its pulse their pulse, its laden body
the mother of their own, its deeps
landscape of their dreams, its monsters
troubling their sleep: it would never let them go.

Did not want to go or come or stay —
and so were human in desire for all there is,
might be, or was, choosing what came nearest
to camels trekking skies, blue and sandy,
windblown, sails over seas heavy
as dunes toppling before winds,
before winds' immense pressure
borne of earth's turning, moon's pull,
light, compulsion of dark powers
crouched in the bushes of space,
to ponder absolutes beyond time and motion,
uttering their beautiful, cacophonous syllables
toward tongues of flame in worlds of wind and light,
while the ocean mutters in its restless bed:
come home, come home, it's late, it's late, it's late.

Declaration of Presence

Last night a bird entered my dream
    not in flight but laid in a carton,
    bony mandible tucked in feathers
    where tiny jewel of eye
    sparkled its intensity of alertness —

to what: captivity? deprivation
    of the spacious air?
    to an alien presence ambiguous as heaven?
    to immobility, as in a coffin?
    to numbing fear?

If Adam's dream was true
    I have no need of dreams,
    all that is not dream you:
    you surround me, you
    shore me up with lap, lap,
    the work of breast, and rip-rap of chat,
    you constellate my nights
    with all the houses I might ever need,
    even in sleep you murmur
    breath's declaration of presence that is you.

So real, if ever bird enter
    I will have slept in creation's hand
    that from my cage released you
    to make a world

of incandescent spirit,
simple earth and water,

and the winged words
that call into being
our life.

Gogmagog

for Charlotte and Colin

Light years away some small blue planet
turns a moving face to dark,
and sends by blip or esp or other sign.

Bent toward dark and dense,
heavy-heavy, gravity's immense grip,
grasps light's lightness, stills its waves,
till holding can no longer hold.

A surge, intense, glows pulse
from core-mass-heat toward cooler edge,
in amnions of aether, fire and fission,
engendering light, lightning, life,

love on some small planet, incontinent,
that births moon or moons,
makes out of time tides, its color blue,
and turns a moving face to light.

To Isabel Allende with Many Thanks!

Back from New York and *Anna Christie*
to a mailbox full of a week's detritus
and *Of Love and Shadows* in its plain brown wrapper
even the female carrier subliminally guessed
what treasure lay within, placed with care
between two bundles of first-class mail and,
I like to think, closed with a kiss the metal lid securely
that it might be safe this baby on the porch
till our return to bring it in and bring it up—
or it bring us up, to some degree approach its insight,
sympathy, power, and compassion
for what we all were or might have been
and in our dreams still are.

CELEBRATIONS

Celebration

How you make the world shake and glow,
more beautiful your steps from room to room
than moving leaves and all the pacing stars.
You are more changeable than air, more certain
than sunrise. When birds sing, comfortable
in their morning drowse, you snuggle down,
warm in cocoon of blankets while I wait
for the butterfly start of your day.
Lighthearted, you lift the clouds. Everything,
entranced by radiance deeper than waves
in ceaseless motion from Aldebaron and beyond,
before the high altar of common day
elevates you, calm in your entirety
as the ocean, while I, all your big and little fish, and I
your attendant moon, and weather of all your reaches,
are set by you in whatever temper to suit a mood,
pacific or typhoon, undulant to every need,
turning as the world unrolls you, panoramic
to dazzled eyes of gods and men, and your man, me.

On a Wave Arrives

That animated face
so smiles we seldom use
the little while it takes
to notice how eyes,
too, beguile the sane,
cautious, staid, sobriety,
our stratagem to keep
all liveliness away
till, flashing from the steep
brow into our anxiety
her feeling enters
moves a part
of us with a speed
and grace as if Athene's
own, bursting from the god's
head, coruscating in a shell,
we abide by yet another
god's way beyond
our dreary dailyness
toward upland, alpine meadows,
peaks the clouds slide by,
and look to see her shell
breast, as it always does,
the mothering seas,
she rising over the last wave in,
her nipples half revealed
beneath the foam,
fountains her radiance.

Given, the Female

There were two of them anyway, with tongues and all.
She for a time was satisfied
with "yes," later acquiring "no" and "not now,"
while male words, prolific as fleas,
hurled themselves through the garden like sleet.

"It's the moon and I am full," she said,
no harvest, even if the hay hangs thick scented,
as if a balloon rising carried in its hot center
the exhalations of pain, frustration, and desire,
as if an ocean, bedded in the center of the world,
heaved its mass and moaned for her
around the edges of its rocky shores.
It is the moon full in a whiteness
circled with darkness,
red at the unhealed suture—
sick for that, are the men.
The wind of their voices winds down
from heights. Howling under the moon,
they prowl, and sniff, and titivate,
till it sinks beyond the sea
taking the tide.

A Penny from the Old Guy

To find a penny in the street
    is her delight,
more than she can utter—
    but laughs and jumps
and does a little jig.

So much joy so cheap
    that periodically
I seed the gutter.

The Daughter as Given

Given, yes, or come by—as if by chance,
except in love's lottery nothing is by chance,
but fixed, determined from the beginning of time,
its time. There are any number of times,
perhaps infinite, for any number of worlds,
every world full of daughters,
struggling to be born from the daughters
of other daughters, or adding a father,
of which a girl cannot have too many—
daddy, pop, meany, sir, old bastard,
sugar daddy, each like a vitamin
with his special contribution to the system.
Too much of any one is a poison, too little
and the darling languishes
or goes tough as a callous from too much resistance.

The case of second fathers is special:
going in where she came out is an incest
certified by law, and sanctioned
by impulse of body to be everywhere at once.
There is a principle—the equal distribution
of material good—that covers the case.
And another—the universal right
of spiritual access—that sanctions it.

If there are two daughters, that makes the case
even more special, and four, phenomenal.
So many mothers and daughters is a full measure:
mothers are whole, fathers
can be sub-divided. Each part leaps up,
half fulfilled, half deprived, and in the long run
half crazy—as befits a man in company
of so many beloveds.

Gathering and Going

She moves out of the past still alive,
eight children behind, going their own ways,
down the long hill, over the bridge,
the water below silted, slow,
along the dusty, weed-high road
to clattering wood planks across a tributary,
turns left, moves down the right bank into woods
out of warm morning sunlight into shade,
clumps of ferns still folded
in the gloom of left-over night.

The birds forage like us . . .
stoops to gather greens,
puts them in a basket.
The voice from her bonnet calls out:
Edith, Hazel, Carrie, Laura, Clifford, Rose!
—Alice, find Howard!

In the shadows, in the deep brush,
they are secret as the woodthrush and phoebe,
all but the list of their voices lost.
I look at the gossamer dandelion head
held in my hand like a ring for bubbles.
A vapor trail divides the evening sky.
Feathery seeds blow into the still air.

Gates

When to press passion
in record breaking curl,
love flexes lifting muscle
and brings all strength
all purpose and design
to bear on knotted heart,
there's no room
on that instant jewel
for other turn
than this dance of angels
leaping beyond stars
at motion's height
moving through heaven's gate
where in his place a haloed Peter
from that eminence judges
all entrances.

Farther then
than any joy-flung lark
has love lifted me
to make the milky way
there where it runs
across exclamatory skies
a glittering stream
of our confluence
flaming at Peter's foyer

aspiring to be graced
by God of life
in all our little
and our greater loves.

Go to any place we meet—
by rocks, on grass,
in water, not too cold
to chill our rising heat,
there mingle breath,
and other things
too tedious to relate,
as we no more grow old:
at stand,
time's still.

Trespass and Transfiguration
Kehoe Beach

for Cheryl

Around the breast-shaped rise of land
four Holsteins meander.
One gazes out over the pulse of sea
or mildly yearns toward hands to ease them.
They have paused
at the rim of a missing shape.
My companion murmurs,
I love those cows.

Which Year

for Queen Anne

Whatever curve your scapula
    that covers, as a hand,
      surges of elation, tightened breath,

whatever verve
    of bone and ligament
      guides flesh through urgencies of want,

whatever sundering
    your nurture's nacre encloses
      to make of loss perfection's round,

what metamorphoses
    breasts lobed
      of budded lotus take,

are lineaments of you—
    whole, inseparable plenitude
      providing us beloveds endless suck.

Whatever year, it makes no difference,
    you here now
      are dearest luck.

Janus-wise

for Melissa

Born into the month
that is a door from
past to future, you
survey with cool gaze
the enigma, time,
that makes darling
girls haughty with years
soon become naughty
by lakes under moon-
light and, what is worse,
probably join some
sorority whose
motto is love Jews
until their bones crack,
a goyische ploy—

survey, to be sure,
also your handsome
lad, leaning to look
deep into the eyes—
oh Bella Donna!—
of one frail vessel
after another,
wondering if some
fine day he might fall

into those manholes
that have drowned cooler
types—God save the Mark!—
but never turn
a hair of that trim
coiffeur, for it is
evident that you
are blessed in your birth-
day with protectors:
tonight Moliere,
on Sunday, Chekhov,
Calderon de la
Barca, and Franklin,
while tomorrow gives
Sontag and Riding,
and two who give too
to this your birthday
the gift of their lives
kept whole in their books—
Spenser's high romance,
Gibbon's history—
to keep you Janus-
like, both young and wise.

What I Haven't Learned
from Jonquils

Last winter at the end
precocious jonquils sprang
out of leaf mold,
nakedness a shame
to dormant trees, shrubs and grass.
Waiting for the vernal right
I covered them with leaves.

This year bolder by a week,
they flaunt green out of deep snow.
Winds toss their crazy blades, frost bites.
I, by the fire,
warm my cautious bulbs.

SPIRITS OF PLACES

Gardens

for Katherine Crewe

Gardens there are of mind, terrain, and myth
God given or, by whatever instrument of grace,
transported from depots of paradisal parts

to gentle thought, wilderness, to make
luxuriant the fantasies of some former place
known as if inherent in the DNA,

birthmap or sign or palimpsest of truth.
This is not in question, what is is this:
the sound of water running through a vast

cave, its many streams, a pool's black
depth softened by light to deep blue,
shapes moving there, living darts

of silver, and a sound as if rocks
breathed. This too: grass reaching to a sky
through which wings flew, and rocking clouds,

no sound but the look of golden grain waving
on stems of straw that glowed along their length,
up from earth neither hot nor cold.

And this: forsythia in rows in bloom,
a figure in a gown of white with blue darts,
three columns casting purple shadows on

a lawn that slopes to sand and breaking water
and a figure, naked, looking out to sea
and nothing, nothing but the water moves.

Take These Pictures

standing vigilant as hosts
to put us at our ease.
They seem to ask what we would like.
We stammer something:
oh, whatever you have.
They, hospitable always,
enigmatic,
do not immediately respond,
give us what they have,
which may be, after all,
what we did not know we wanted,
that now we think we cannot live without.

Paintings on the Wall

How soon what we love dissolves—
sunlight, shadows in the grass, grass—
that you recall for us
in tongue your makers
learned from mutterings,
if only a syllable or so,
of what came down in whole
sentences from the caves at Lascaux,
in which no gutteral of hatred
was yet, after eons, uttered:
only life to celebrate,
on their victims life bestow
in form and tint,
scant measures of their life's intent
to sketch beyond the instant
likeness of a world
living as they made it up,
at which we gaze, hoping to find what we do not
    know
is forever gone.

Only pictures we have made
in our most innocent hours approximate
a world we recognize—and lucky the day
a stroke, a beam, a wink of light
solicits from some niche or cave

a gesture of response to say
we painted with our love
what we have had to kill
and all things of the world in which we take delight.

It is then with silence most acute
of line and shape and color that you seem to speak
to us, no longer deaf, no longer mute.

The Watching Tree

A tree watches my thoughts
  whose own are twigs and branches and leaves
  and a trunk full of history:
  of droughts, wet-years, fire, the boring worm.

A tree watches—how, I do not know.
I have tried to catch a pin oak monitoring
  as it stands by my bedroom,
  largest of its kind for miles,
whose syphons of analysis must be visible
  if I look long enough.   I stand under it, searching
  till the squirrels are angry with me.

Once I climbed into its branches.
At twenty feet, there was a nail driven into the trunk.
Nails do not travel in trees—
  someone had been there before me.
Was that nail a threat against oaks
  prying into thought, a sentence of axing?

No tree is a stranger,
  seems always to have known me.
I would not like to have to choose one
  to stand against and be shot—

unless the choosing could go on forever,
until I dropped of old age,
like a dead branch.

Perhaps I am choosing: as I pass a tree
   I survey its shape, the texture of its bark,
   the leaves, the twigs, and how the branches range.

They may have something to tell me,
   but what, they do not say.

Sheep Dogs

I have never been in Clifden, Connemara.
If I might, I'd ask the sea
why it stays so far away,
and why it lets the rocks
hold up the shore.

There'd be an answer—
sea's never mum,
always whispering something
or shouting in a tantrum.
Thing is, to train the ear:

We're hooked on sound
drugged in our mother's stream
and love the lapping waters
we know we've always missed,
love the round effrontery
of words' tumbling ear-ripe
in the boozy dark,
where to live is to get pissed
listening to stories
without much point.

Did you go to Connemara?
No, he said, I went to Wicklow.
Did you see a pony show?

Yes, he said.
And what were they like?
I don't know, he said,
there were these sheep dogs.

What are those horses called?
Percherons.
The Normans caught a stud at Voville,
I think it was, or Deauville,
—no, that's in the north—
when Martel hammered the Saracens.
And after the crusades
some brought back Arabian stallions
to Perche, and mated them
        with the Voville line, or the Deauville line.
Fifty generations in that climate
—look what it did to men—
labor and limestone soil,
and what do you have?—Percherons.

That's horseshit.
The Percheron is primitive French.
Arabian breeders say
the speckled hides
of Percherons are not
the true, oriental, "flea-bitten" grey.
There are two kinds,
the little Percheron
and the big.
The stud book keeps them pure:

Did you ever see a middle-sized Percheron?
I never saw a little one.

Look at that, I said.
You call that wrestling?
He's not stomping his head,
he's stomping the mat.
You're right, he said—
that's show biz.

If they had gone
to Clifden, Connemara,
when the light of Irish history
clove Clifden from the sea,
gold where it rose, on houses white
and pink. . . .
Celtic light, ray after ray,
made day the Roman night
and Frankish oblivion.
Irish singers, caught proleptic
having sent, sing anyway
along the broken walls and hedgethorn
down the valleys of the Boyne and Avonmore.

Oira di Crevoladossola

Wine

Distant peaks circle with snow
Oira's gardens and willow rows.

Vines along the sun slopes show
fat buds, down reapers' swaths flows

May crop of flowers and grass.
Mountain shadows in the pass

move toward north's high colder mass,
the Alpine glacial morass's

slow dripping and wind's bright chill.
In cantinas, ferments still

for a few days autumn's juice,
bittering. Decanted twice

into jugs, the nectar grows
red as sunset storms, bestows

a power the gods thought death
defying, as if one's breath,

shorn from the nourishing vine,
were made into immortal wine.

Evening settles still and cold
over Oira, night time's old

legends coalesce in smoke—
witchcraft, the crow's morning stroke—

rolls, ricotta, glasses set,
wine poured, night passes.

Oira di Crevoladossola

Places of Worship

A woman's wavy scythe is swung
to lay the sweet stems low.
She points to her stylish scarecrow,
whether one asks or not:
I too make art.

The witch whose house is up the slope
reads palms, interprets signs,
and lays a curse on anyone
who laughs at her or counterfeits
her secret lore.

While Kali in her studio,
three easels on the go,
to Feldman on a cassette tape
paints houses, mountains, streets, skies—but
no human part.

The priest, whose church on top the height
he claims by seniority,
will not give up the sinecure
nor sanction any rite but his
one day a week.

Rooms where Tadeo presses out
the whey fill with steam.
He cleans the gleaming copper vat's
sheen even shinier
with large red hands.

In Marcolina's house behind
the church, the shelves are stacked
with poetry, walls hung with art,
glass cabinets are full
of porcelain.

Ken looks at houses falling in
and seeks to make them whole
by searching out each rightful heir
according to the code
Napoleon.

When he has found some thirty odd
and signed them to the deed,
in France, in Greece, in Netherlands,
he orders timber and the pipes
to make them new.

The crow is not alarmed by change
and comes to take his bread
each day. Good fortune, says the witch,
to have a crow to feed.
She looks, and smiles.

Summer's early light glows green on
Crevoladossola's
nearest slopes, pink on distant snows.
Crow, darkest at the prime,
alights and crows.

Oira di Crevoladossola

Houses

Decay of a stone house across the way
speaks nevertheless of what we seek
all our days: return to dark stalls
with their posts and lintels, wood withered
by inner weather, withes' smoke, where sky
light, fractured by slanted roofstones' tight
cracks, infinitely slow, moves its bright tracks
over darkened planks toward bed and cover.
The weave of stone from left to right leaves
undone a row five courses up begun
from right to left, twice as long and tight.
Riddle of these tiers cannot be settled,
"Oira" notwithstanding: To this hour
Basques call it "houses". Irigaray asks,
Did one come this way, stay here—dead,
left to generations after, this craft
of stacked walls and roof and the abstract
design of herringbone that is a sign
of life by wool, nets, unending strife
among mountains, tribes, spears always hung,
as these in stone, at ready to be seized,
hurled, signs spread for an unobserving world?
Still, crow, with eyes of other place, knows
cause, knocks at first light, and caws and caws
until his daily bread is laid on sill.

Bread and water will appease the dead,
so Kali thinks. In her two worlds folly
is not to look, not to observe the knots
tied in every skein the three sisters dyed
a hue from past lives, invisible but true—
as crow's knowledge and body's aura shows
beyond the flesh and power to abscond.
Kali paints no mortal form, tallies
in place the shining of a house's face,
its charm, radiance of human karma,
lours, sunk in earth, or rooted, soars.
Scenes, sites, take shape from what is inner seen,
scape of meditation, "Promises" on tape,
heart's metre tripled in the drum-beat parts—
blood surges, and a house seems understood.

Oira di Crevoladossola

Cantina

He fills the fermentation tub knee deep
with plump ripe bunches, south's late sweet growth,
                                                    full,
grey with lace work *muffa nobile*, mashed
by feet trampling skin, pulp, and mold to must.

When night falls, table is set with pasta,
bread, ricotta cheese, and last year's vintage
with such potency, that none knew then, no
one now, whether its virtues come from feet,
grapes—or magic of Oira, Greece, and Spain.

Whatever else there is to know, at best
these hills, witchery-rich, make wine and love
to last without preservative but use.

Thanksgiving

Who's giving thanks for what?
Little Coon's words fall back in his throat.
What is a reservation? Freedom within bounds?
Prison without walls? Shame with its own territory?

Before was deep forest, breadth of ocean.
Out of one came the sick and exhausted,
out of the other strength and knowledge—
of soil, plants that grew there, pumpkin, squash, corn,
berries in marshes, eggs of shore-birds, venison,
oysters, cod and lobster, the turkey.

In colors of autumn, before leaves fell,
pale and bronze feasted together
beneath oaks at the edge of a stream,
spoke the language of signs,
gave cloth and furs, beads and buckskin,
smoked the pipe. Smoke of the fires and pipes
moved in slow spirals.

Grey clouds over the Jemez hint a sparkle of snow
to frost boughs of firs along Garcia Street.
Acequia Madre slumbers, Canyon Road is still.
Not Mary's place.
In steam of cooking, words rise faster than leaves fall.
Whatever else, they say thanks, and mean love.

This is the now of remembrance.
Burn the bitter logs.
Let the wind blow and leaves fall,
as they did, and will.
Let the gifts be given—a kiss, a smile, a hug.
Who are we, to give thanks for more than this?

April and Leaving

Flowering plum that backs Kendall Bell
   between two concrete pylons,
enpurpled, fading with sun
   to pink and white, will soon
smudge to color of regret,
   a muddy ochre. Leaves,
perhaps hoping to stay through wind scythes,
   mimic twig, or bark, or branch,
no less human than place-movers
   who in mortal vortex
with respite to choose,
   would keep place, imperturbable,
rooted, boled, in leafy head
   a brain not roiled
beyond absolutes of wind,
   rain, wimpling snow,
shelter in desolate season,
   or lightning's riddling bolt
that sends without reason
   destruction and ugliness of scarred
bark, trunk, disheveled crown.

   Time with slower lightning
strikes undeterred, relentless,
   all targets—buildings, seas, mountains,
you and me—as bolt the tree,

which even unmarred
will have its wood merge
    with dust, earth, the air,
Till what was massive, solid in our eyes,
    spacious as world they stow
within mind's galaxy,
    becomes wholly transparent,
a rift in continuity of what they
    know as only real,
which memory's second sight, eager
    to reconstruct, re-does, remakes,
reconstitutes the real within a universe
parallel, sequentially permanent in mind and word.

One lives within the other. Force
    goes in and out, language of energy,
motion of love, play of dolphin, whale,
    a place of light re-entering dark
where shade becomes the body of light,
    its paramour.
Hell has heaven, earth cries.

Triple Helix

You suffer from the double helix,
an algia common to people
of talent and sensitivity.

One end of a cone spirals out from us.
What we perceive is the large view
opposite: you, generous, beautiful,
loving us all.

The other cone's end is, you think,
you in its small pointiness.
Its opposite largeness shows,
you think, what should have been:
the great reality of expectation.

You are indeed a helix point,
perpendicular, at the top: here are
base we, and there you,
the pinnacle.

You will not have us so,
but on your side, forming a prop
that makes us go.

May, Maybe

Better you should have failed me,
but were kind (or ever hopeful),
gave me my incomplete.

I learned so much — I learned —
read all the books that I forgot
and turned to your faces in ignorance,
from which I have never forgotten
anything that matters — what,
I do not remember. You are
as you are, the seasons:
a hint of light pouring over clouds,
a stinging wind. . . .

perhaps, perhaps . . . but the best
is here, is right here, is
nothing, as between two hands
where they clasp, two minds when they speak,
the secret rising out of every essay
as I read, to sit on my shoulder,
at the good parts whispering in my ear,
"See? See?"—seldom made me tired.

You often came to slump before me,
ghosts out of midnight hours,
and slept, offering your eyelids
for me to write on,

the cassettes of your ears —
were they ever on record?

Once in three weeks some word, or phrase,
or pattern, would kindle your eyes.
Then I knew, or guessed, what fires
might roar for casting great figures,
kilns white hot for firing the cold clay
you will turn into cities, governments,
families, and humble art.

I wrote "sheep" on the board.
You could only ba-a-a—and get lost.
        Took me back in your arms
        and smiled, as if I had never been gone.

Trio

After August evening in the tatami room
     listening to Smetana's trio
on the death of his daughter,
she four and capable of contrary motion
in scale of C and singing Lieder with texts,

you woke in pre-dawn dark
to a loon's chattering
in the reed bed at lake's edge,
and swam through chill, quiet water
toward the hidden island.
Half way out you turned,
stroked heavily back to shore,
now strange in a colorless mist.

    Calls of that ancient bird,
indecipherable as cries
or silence of human grief's
refusal to be reconciled
to what gives up
without need, or recompense,
justice, bargain, hope, or mercy,
a dear and irreplacable hostage,
echoed over the lake's dark water
till sunrise.

Evening/Lightening

for Penny

A moored sloop, a pyramid
   in pale lavender desert sunset
bring sea and sand together
   (little sand, those million worlds)
in a close nautical arrangement
   —is that an ochre quai stretches between?—
of torn sail and triangle shorn by sheet of light,
   intensity obliterating sight.

Above, a cloud leans, two black boars,
   ears forward, run,
darkness of three thousand years
   over sail and stone and sand
mix with color, innocence of pink, pips of orange,
all sun's incalculable spending.

Streak of lightning rips the center,
   a tentacle, nerve of life, descends,
   falling water from a high place,
   Jacob's ladder, a rigging,
   infinitesimal human semblance climbs
toward the boar's ear, a black hole,
   where the leash is caught.

A thatched cottage leans beyond the pyramid,
    or head and neck of black polled, white banded
    needlebeak, among birds a unicorn, so rare.

Our eyes root in this you gave,
    let inner vision flower
in tiers of light and color
    —we ask your leave
out of love
    that in scraps and tittles, blobs and torn bits
makes home of these particles ingathered
    to the hearth of its chromatic burning,
where we sit, admire you and us and it,
    in a temporal pattern
    of likeness and dissimilitude
for long as last you and us and it,
    burning in the greater fire.

Constant

Light, creation thinking,
enters the simple and the complex:
into dough that rises and bakes,
thus we consume creation's thought.

A sparkle in your friend's eye
is holy light emerging.
Regard it with attention—
it may be the light of your life. Look deep,
receive whatever glint is offered.

Do not close off as a mirror does,
    that reflects back the bright and good,
keeps nothing for itself, flat, cold,
        hard and indifferent.

Be grateful the moon waxes in generosity.
The speed of love is 300,000 km/second.

The Lathe

As flower turns away from plant,
wave from ocean,
our loving in the slant
sunlight turned away
for the loss coming on.

After October's mist closed down,
I left by our track to the stream

away from August places
where strips of canvas
shielded naked bathers,

stood a while to watch the autumn sun
move pale shadows slowly
over frozen grass,
the year turning away.

Woman with Cigarette

The woman in her bed waking
   to a blur of light and wooly shadows
reaches for enormous spectacles
   that bring the blue in clear and deep
above azaleas, roses, violets, and flags.

In printed gown wrapped round
   she wanders out into the yard
among light spears and shadow splashes
   where on a favorite seat of stones
set in a bank of juniper
   takes inventory of what he left:

the moving patterns shaped of sun and shade
   the path of stepping stones
that leads toward a Chinese moon
   of redwood hung in native limestone
opening on a meadow
   where scattered ashes
now come up in pollen dust
   instills the drone of foraging bees
with notions of his cloudy voice
   moving fragments of her memory
to form a garden of its own
   with path of stepping stones
a gate, a field, an urn

seasons of wind and snow
and one of rain
   glinting in each drop like spectacles
flower beds her printed gown

he in the gazebo she designed
   with Japanese tiled roof
took measure of her lavish gifts
   not least herself
that work of time and luck and love.

And as the evening went its way
   down path, through trees, on into distant sky
bees withdrew, the flowers closed,
   and dew, upon the grass, her gown, and spectacles
softened the shape of him
   to blur of light, to drag of shade, to sunset tone.

Still and All

"AFTER THE HOLOCAUST ONLY SILENCE IS APPROPRIATE"

After the many voices silenced—
    the millions
whose simple goodmorning, goodnight,
would never stir the air
in bedrooms and kitchens—
                to keep silent,
to offer no word of comfort and affection,
to be an accomplice in that negation—no!

We speak: "Good morning, good night,
I love you, sleep well."

                They come back to us.

PRESENT OR ACCOUNTED FOR

Airborne Man

Where, oh where, has Miller gone,
with his Harris cut short
and his tale left long?
In what bedroom after Pinehurst—
jump boots gleaming on the sill,
jacket with a single stripe flung on chair,
his Lovely stretched out,
sung along his staff in all the keys major
that first night of morning snow and toast—
did he hang his unicorn?
After, in a minor mode, tears salt to kill,
wove him through the openings of her loom,
and on the third day, as the moon
rose over U-boat lairs, sent him
filled with joy and doom
to war in cocky hat, his shining boots, and patch.

One waved a green-back flag
above his head in the PX bar,
fat lips and finger nose, a ghetto grin.
He gave no sign—even at friendship's scowl,
screwed into the eyebrow's thick black line—
back to barracks took his unicorn.
This was how he checked his 'chute:
turned three times the ring in,
three times out, to fix the Star.

After many a summer dies the swan,
among other creatures at bloat

in February rain. My lads collect
pictures, statuary, and polish coffee urns,
candlesticks, repair cuckoo clocks,
you wrote, letter of February one,
Headquarters Company, 69th Infantry.
When the weather picks up will
throw themselves heartily in-
to floral arrangements.
Deposed, also, that your Carbine
Calibre .30 M1, had one round in chamber,
you didn't know how to get it out:
McClellan was a long time ago.

Dear Corporal (yours of April first,
pulling rank) today in a German village,
house of a music teacher, busts
of Beethoven and Bach, but no
Gershwin or Berlin. Wunderlich,
hunched over the keys, beer stein on lid,
played blues: it was Casablanca,
he was playing it.
I got your letter. Good to know
for a few moments that you were alive.
The Old Sarge.

Write again why don't you? Didn't I?
Is Society Hill better for what you did?
And if you died? The Directory does not
say. What happened with the round,
your Lovely, mine, and me?

Parable of the Cave
(in a small cafe)

Clear faded blue on tan skin,
    the number of your fate.

Breached from piles of bones
    to live in tents

was paradise enough: love,
    birdsong, morning light

and music cast a spell
    untrancing death. . . .

Our numbers not so blue,
    and paradise in cheaper goods—

pancakes, coffee, and service
    in a small warm room—

until like thunder
    from clear skies

you thrust the number
    at our eyes.

Shadows, flesh, and fire
    strike us from our concentration.

a small poem for a small boy

for Joseph Brandon Tomlins

First a nipple on the world
to suck dry before it goes away
feel of her, warm, close, and milk

then you see, beyond the soft rise,
shapes that swoop and fly away—
the face of her you will never
stop loving, the face of him
you will someday hate

later you find out that's the way it is
and he will come down again in dreams
like a god

and touch, the comforter,
a nipple that you own,
and hearing, that pounds at your head
with bang do this and bang do that

meanwhile people tell you
and tell you how much you have to learn
—and to behave, behave, behave

all you can do is
try to be yourself
—and you won't know who that is.
bon voyage!

The Architect

Reading Heidegger, December '91

"LITTLE KNOWLEDGE, BUT MUCH JOY IS GIVEN TO
MORTALS. . . ."
                                                    Hölderlin

Heidegger in the hut above Todnau
had reached the height of his grey-green thinking
on *Dasein*, time, and being—and the word.
If he had then come on to Mt. Snefels
what buff and umber insights might have flared
over the raw force of uranium:
the ultimate design of Being, why
it does not matter that *Das Nichts nichtet.*

"Poems of the true poet are poems
of homecoming." The master-builder, too,
the *archetekton* of materials,
thinks toward home through memory and desire:

Mt. Snefels, looming north of Telluride,
the Uncompahgre Forest and Plateau,
Dolores waters holding Naturita,
all that arid upland, in a calyx
long flowering out of the Molas Di-
vide towards her deep love the Colorado.

What you desire is what's revealed, the myth
the telling word, memory, the thinking
back. Without both, you were a sign not read,
and homeless in an empty land, you would
not know where you are, or who, or why.

You have structured the *extases* of time,
past alive in present, *future* to be
born—as when in Denver's Tabor Center
the modes were re-arranged for you and Lynne.
Strange, mysterious freedom, within walls!

Those who did not go to school—Gropius,
Le Corbusier, Mies van der Rohe—
and some who did, including John Novack,
drew on van der Rohe, original
a source as Gaudi, and as authentic
in the modes of time.
                    Authentic present
as a now for Novack stands at fifty,
divide spectacular as the Dallas.

From Third Park's bluffs and thunders flares the word.
Dasein is being there and being here
in vision, function, form, materials.
To make the perfect bell, sent out of tune
by dustings of snow, is the builder's fate.
Memory of what was restrains desire
for what is. You build, snow falls: you know this
in hate, in love, in anguish, in living.

Virginia Woolf, 28 March 1941

All the early photos show a thin, drop-
shouldered sibling to a sturdy sister,
goddess, it is clear, of art and love,
while she with bandy arms
seems dinging out some skewer
for self-torture, shaped like Greek,
King Edward on the haft.

At the death, Prometheus with a rock,
eagles at the brain for ages,
a second time into the water
to become a fin somehow
—as fin she is,
cutting through the deep of every mind
that reads: a rite of passage
true and faltering as her steps
into the thirty-three year waters
of the voyage out.

To Jennifer

[Fr. *fer,* from Lat., *ferrum,* iron, hence Iron Jenny—by
extension "Jennifer the Strong"]

In Normandy, from which (I like to believe)
"Jennifer" derives, women are like apples,
tasty on the limb, delicious on the ground.
Once plucked, they ripen though many lives
as girl-child, coquette, lover, wife, and mother,
sometimes mistress—of herself and of no other.
To this traditional *arc-en-ciel* she adds a span
as woman of the world, and work, profession,
and professor of the values man once thought secure
as his by right of primogeniture.

God's second thought, on seeing that Her first, a man,
failed as *mensch,* was Eve,
though not a *mensch,* a *macher.*
God, seeing she was good and man was weird,
gave to him a beard, to her a child—
whose retrospective name was "Adam".
And She said, "Oi, veh!,
"already I should make her in my image first."
Improving on the model, (somewhat wild),
She came to Jennifer and stopped.
"God knows," She said, "I don't know why
perfection is my goal:
what's for Vanessa left to try?" And so she copped.
And so She broke the mold.

His Firm Estate

Mr. Eikenberry

He liked the quiet of his common flat,
shades drawn against the Oklahoma light.
tonight's game would field the Cardinals
against the Cubs. Schoendienst would play,

a name to fit the German of his own
from Iowa. Game done, the shambling king
was haled into his head: town, state
and whirling orb were drawn into an order

of mind that held more things than are dreamed
in our philosophy, yet simple as a star,
held in such motion that we knew
if ever power were in single man

this is our prince time could not hold, nor place
nor platitude still his reigning mind.

On the Avenue

The boy in the field
was catching flies.

He wanted a fungo bat
with his name burned in
to knock the ball into the air
and catch it himself before it fell.

That was more difficult
than seeing his face
in profile.

He wanted to pitch the ball
and hit his own slider
over the fence.

He would collect a little sweat
from his cap and grip the ball
with thumb and two fingers.

He would lean back
lift a foot higher than his head
swing the arm through
and let go with a wrist snap.

As the spinning spheroid cut
the corner of the plate
his bat would meet it
with a solid crack.

That was harder than flying
off the garage roof.

He would like to be the umpire
calling himself safe at home
as he slid in a tick ahead
of the ball.

He would snag his own line drive
over third with a backhand stab
and catch himself off first.

He wants a glove and a bat
he wants a ball
and cleats.

He wants to give himself
these things.

His Own Stunts

for Darcy

A man is laying bricks for a patio,
The herring-bone is difficult and goes awry.
He is insatiable for accuracy—takes
The bricks up and puts them down,
For the sake of tightness packs the sand
into the cracks. His hands are bloody
Where the sharp shards bite in:
He is doing it himself.

A man is cutting dead limbs out of a tree.
It is an oak, full of knots, the wood is tough.
He trims branches back smooth to the trunk's ragged
    bark.
The large limbs he puts in a sling
To lower through the tangle of smaller boughs.
He clambers like a goat
To find a dead branch hidden behind the bole.
His neighbors are tiny with big eyes.
The world lies all around him.

A man is telling a story.
He is sitting on his bedroll.
They see his mouth shape words in the light.
Silent, his lips go on moving as the flames flicker.

His story is about long nights in another place
Where he wanted to live. The sea was near,
Stars hung under the clouds. The air is still.
His eyes look through the fire to some far place
As he comes to the end, doing it himself.

Dwight Nicholson, Here

for Jane

Did you begin in childhood
with Jane's elegant arches
that led two beyond singularities
and the clutter of humanized landscape
to planetary vistas,
the invisible mathematics of space-time,
and a final arch,
through which you passed
with creation's primal power,
going on, know from the beginning
no end of curves and curving,
of the finite one the infinity?

ii
If three giant spikes
were driven into earth's crust
at Racine, Iowa City, and Tulsa,
the salty edges of this land
would rise dripping out of the seas
and let their waters roar
toward the center
over layers of heated granite,
boiling basalt,
force steam to blow
through chimneys in dormant cones,

thick mists lowering
from Sierras to Wichitas
from Blue Ridge to Ozarks,
there could be no more lamenting
than for what was possible,
no less celebration for what is.

Incontinent sorrow will not balance so.

iii
At festival requiem,
when gaudy and grey
survive in the colors of evening,
when ptarmigan and snowshoe
white with whirling flakes,
unsighted beneath drifted brush,
hear in the wind chorus and a solo owl
benighted winter's loss and grief,
the only comfort is what
in all the coming has come to be,
not the memory or images of desire,
not letters or the taped voice,
nor the lost
in any of its phantom forms,
only the going on:
to have come through the arches,
to suffer the long tears,
and the ceaseless ache, and the void,
having come and gone,
to live in the ongoing—
as you do, if you ever did.

Intermezzo

When the wig fell
    off your cobalt ravaged skull
and half the tatty night-gown slipped
    to reveal a lank bosom,
you were at your best.

A quirky smile said
    what can I do,
eyes twinkled with a grin
    you may even have felt.

Mean it you did,
    as desperate ransom
for the body's gone beauty,
    a way of flirting
with what was left.

The Living Art of Virginia

She laid down the objects of her concern
around the walls—sketches and notebooks,
scores stratified on the piano lid,
the Moog layered with ideographs and charts,
journals piled ziz-zag, with a weathered look—
all things that time and life and art might use
    some day
or she, to improvise a theme in lights, a play,
whatever: stages on the way. To where?
Someplace we could not expect.

*What is it that we learn
inhibits learning anything else?*

In a garden chair among her beds of herbs and bulbs
she named each box and piece of paper,
when it was empty, when it was blank—
and who filled it.
Anamnesis: she redeemed the times,
especially the syncopated ones.

As we unpacked the small room's brain,
imago of a brain,
branching and building its covert awareness,
it took on a life of its own.

It comes in a kind of knowingness . . .
all the levels, these different kinds of energies
enter the mind,
several energy systems happening at the same time,

happened to the arms and legs
that moved this load of living Tulsa,
moving in its own imaginative might
(though we strained, or thought we did)
filled the vans and car trunks,
organized its own parade,
down Fifteenth Street.
What a low life was entered into
in that place off Delaware—
as if a rich, expansive universe
imploded, now all its shards packed in,
a dusty concentrate—all these different
kinds of energies at shabby rest—
until they resurrected at her death.

She had learned something—knew that,
and said it—that kept her from learning
    something else,
but learned that something less than most,
and practiced all her life unlearning it:
Schoenberg?—What was the matter
with me? Two hundred candles, circled,
give a soft answer: nothing.

The event referred to in the poem was the removal of Living Arts files, memorabilia, furniture, and works of art from the room in Virginia's garage on Oswego to the apartment west of Delaware provided by the University of Tulsa for storage of these materials. The last lines refer to the circles of candles at TuCCA with a pair of Virginia's shoes at the center. The italicized lines, spoken by her, are taken from the video shown during the evening of February 14, 1991, with some minor changes. The opening, as will be recognized by anyone who had seen them, refer to the main rooms in Virginia's house.

Nicole/Nicole

You were for mother, father,
the living text in which their subtexts
figured now, then, here, there—
and finally not at all,
though yours in them
still tells the hours
as surely on Montmartre
toll the bells of Sacré-Coeur.

The shining city claims
in all its ancient, youthful guises—
twisted, spacious, colorful and grey—
your colors threaded through the quarters,
weft among its many walks and walkers
of a world on fire, troubled and glorious,

makes your brief world Paris,
embraced in round, complete,
whole within its borders, you,
beginning to end.   Recording so
all steps and streets, confront
a mystery with humble knowledge,
the city's pattern a cipher of your life
spirited and still, partial and entire:

On the Pont de la Tournelle
looking wide to Notre Dame,
you have seen the river boats
leave their wakes on either side.

On the Pont du Carrousel
see how slow from Pont des Arts
go waters of the Seine, serene
in their unceasing flow.

Each citizen and *étrangere*
crossing boulevard and square
encounters in the misty air,
or bright, an essence of Brumaire,
young, brusque—not debonnaire,
caring, as if hurt were care,
faring through brown leaves, bare boughs
towards Spring's slow power of repair
in warmth, in light, in flower.

Whatever love is
strikes stormy-jubilant as March,
warblers fling black and rainbow colors
where a few late winter bent stalks stilt
among the splattered, matted leaves
in the garden of the Tuilleries
—still burning in this long, slow fire.

Red birds, as they build their nests, sing
"no better, no better, no better,"
and sky lets down its sodden clouds
over roofs, and twigs, and cobblestones.

A hurdy-gurdy down the street
 winds morning into noon,
what's left of last night's moon nods overhead,
 in Parc Monceau the great trees creak
above the Chinese bridge's arc,
 while back and forth a walker weaves
 within the city's selvedge
of remembered selves
 the patterns that a lifetime leaves
out of living, out of dark.

Nicole was in her early twenties when she died in a Paris apartment house fire.

The Students Who Died

we talked of Plato and the Cave
the coming through to light
your eyes kindled
sometimes you must have napped, I did,
or nearly, going on through warm hours
to shape new formulations for my own sake
     the old for you fresh as first sight

in couplets quatrains all the guardian forms
torrents of free verse
prose's multitudinous, rational propositions
  plodding along,
     its rare four-legged gallop

sometimes laughter bubbled from your lungs
sometimes you rejected everything
sometimes I wished you gone
    sometimes you left

sometimes I call the roll
Michael, William, Dianne, Mark, Eden. . . .

Ikon

to Fran

These images from photographs
are most unlike you in their fixity
an iron quiet that does not become you
nor have you ever been so still of lip and limb
but in motions all your own that are metaphors
of mind speaking through the body
lyric messages, all poetry
in the ultimate sense that senses
are the tongues of thought
to say what otherwise stays mute
in the wanting seas that surge
and surge again for consummation
with sun and wind to quicken,
to make the least quiver
that signals life in foam and light,
the ancient inclination to move,
join, enter, and increase
the plasm of being
which you the mother and lover are:

See in these photos how you cuddle and cuff
and, having sent into the world your cubs
spiffed and licked, must take us all
into your guardian circle to bring us up
or as in love to bring us down,

which is your climate, love, intemperate and moist,
ideal for rearing, and for sending forth
into the deserts this green earth
(ourselves and you)
is ever tending to—

See, too, how you make the Brechtian circles close
and in a drama not your own but all yours
act each part as we the motions make
and stiffly strut the parts that you would have us
dance,
you orbiting from wing to wing to cheer us on
—on, you always are, even in sleep
struggling with the demons of desertion,
tyranny, and fear, yourself Prometheus

on this desert rock for our sakes
who profit daily from your gift of fire—

to see at last beyond and through these pictures
—student, mother, actor, editor, and Fool—
essence of so rare humanity
that we mistrust eyes' evidence
what we think we know, and intuition,
because all tell us that this beautiful
imperfect form is Fran our love and friend
and that our love and friend's this form,
but she through every tone and gesture
tells us something else—
that she in each of us and through our lives

has presence as if only so,
and this cannot be caught in photographs,
extension of herself through you and me and those,
and all others that are changed through us by her,
too large for any camera, except perhaps this room
that registers our looks and thoughts,
on some such paper,
in more spacious words than these.

For the Life and Work of Ivar Ivask

Heard when leaves fail, filling the air with falling
Tones like grace notes turned in a slow pavane, the
Music dulls—these chords of the dying year sink
    Low in a dying

Fall: the drum-beat blood in its diastolic
Half-dirge bears her down to the underworld of
Winter, slow her heart in its cave—it stays the
    Running of fountains.

Still, her voice breaks loneliness, cries profoundest
Grief, and trees shake down in regret their last few
Leaves, while he wraps winter around his head and
    Grieves for her weeping

Ivar's loss, makes song which through winter-stricken
Sullen heart flakes petals in flower storms, in
Star falls light words showering deserts—mountain
    Forest and prairie

Surge as seas their burgeoning waves the songs of
Ivar, live in Orpheus, strung to sound on
Arc of death-deaf flesh the rebounding pulses'
    Sensual music.

ABOUT THE AUTHOR

Poetry editor of *Nimrod*, formerly associate editor of *The Hopkins Review*, Manly Johnson has published poems and translations in a variety of journals and little magazines. He has taught at Johns Hopkins, Williams College, the University of Michigan, and The University of Tulsa, with publications about Australian novelists and poets. Hadassah Press and the riverrun press have published two chapbooks of his poetry, and the Frederick Ungar Publishing Company his book about Virginia Woolf. His favorite sports are wrestling, about which he has written, and baseball, which he has coached at the college level. He lives and works in Tulsa with his wife, Francine Leffler Ringold and their circle of friends.